CHINESE FOLK SONGS
COLLECTION

24 TRADITIONAL FOLK SONGS FOR INTERMEDIATE LEVEL PIANO SOLO 中國民歌選曲

ARRANGED BY JOSEPH JOHNSON

ISBN 978-1-4234-6547-8

HAL•LEONARD®
CORPORATION
7777 W. BLUEMOUND RD. P.O. BOX 13819 MILWAUKEE, WI 53213

In Australia contact:
Hal Leonard Australia Pty. Ltd.
4 Lentara Court
Cheltenham, Victoria, 3192 Australia
Email: ausadmin@halleonard.com.au

Visit Hal Leonard Online at
www.halleonard.com

PREFACE

China is a large country inhabited by many people of many different backgrounds and ethnicities. What constitutes China and the Chinese is similar to other large nations. Defined boundaries and peoples are ever changing. These songs represent the Chinese of modern China, of which the Han represent the largest ethnic majority.

Choosing and qualifying folk songs as "popular" or "typical" is a daunting task complicated by the many different languages and cultures that make up the country. In this collection I have chosen to arrange songs popular to Mainland Chinese with the help and guidance of Wen Guo Yao, to whom this collection is dedicated, and her daughter Shen Wen, my wife.

I also received additional help from Jerry Huang on Taiwanese folksongs. I would also like to thank the Deng family for their recommendations concerning familiar tunes, and finally I would like to thank Jennifer Linn for her guidance on this project.

ABOUT THE ARRANGER

Joseph Johnson received his bachelor's degree in music composition with distinction from New England Conservatory of Music where he studied with Robert Ceely and John Harbison. Mr. Johnson has taught for Massachusetts Institute of Technology, Emerson College, Brandeis University and New England Conservatory of Music. Before moving to St. Louis in 2007, Mr. Johnson worked as music director at Christ Church, Waltham, Massachusetts and organist at First Church in Malden, Massachusetts. Mr. Johnson has had over forty performances of his music compositions in the last ten years including works for the concert hall and for church.

Mr. Johnson is currently completing his PhD in composition and theory at Brandeis University. In addition to teaching at the university level, Mr. Johnson taught piano lessons at Music 101 in Melrose, Massachusetts and tutored music theory at the Dana Hall School of Music in Wellesley, Massachusetts.

TABLE OF CONTENTS

ENGLISH TITLE	CHINESE CHARACTERS	PINYIN

NOTES ON THE CHINESE FOLK SONGS

MOUNTAINTOP VIEW (page 7)

The view from Yi Meng Mountain is beautiful. Below you see the river and the fields, which makes for a good harvest. With plenty of food this is a good place to live. This Han song is from Shandong province.

LOVE SONG OF THE PRAIRIE (page 8)

This song is about a beautiful girl. Her face is like the red sun, and her eyes are like the moon. All who pass by her tent turn their heads to admire her beauty. A man wants to give up all his money to become a shepherd and follow her. This song comes from Qinghai province in western China and is sung by Han people—the largest ethnic group in China.

RUNNING HORSE MOUNTAIN (page 9)

This beautiful Han love song is from Sichuan province.

GIRL'S LAMENT (page 10)

Love is the theme of many songs of people all around the world. This Han song from Shaanxi province describes the effects of love on a girl. Because of love she cannot eat or sleep, and her tears drop into her food bowl.

WEDDING VEIL (page 11)

This Uyguhr song is from Xinjiang province. In it the groom petitions his bride, "let me take off your veil so I can see your face!"

SAD, RAINY DAY (page 12)

"Sad, Rainy Day" is about a person out in the rain with no umbrella. The person exclaims, "how pathetic I am!" This Han song is from Guangdong province.

THE SUN CAME UP HAPPY (page 13)

Different adversities make the protagonist of this song upset, but the sun keeps him happy. This Han song is from Sichuan province.

WA-HA-HA! (page 14)

The title of this fun song comes from nonsense syllables sung in a manner similar to fa-la-la-la-la in "Deck the Halls." "Wa-ha-ha!" sings the praise of the country with beautiful imagery—"Our country is a garden with many smiling children." This song comes from Xinjiang province in eastern China and is sung by the Uyghur people.

WHITE FLOWER (page 15)

The Hmong people sing this song in Guizhou province. Men and women sing together and ask each other questions about love.

GREAT WALL (page 16)

This song is sung from a woman's perspective, lamenting her life without her husband who is away from home working to build the Great Wall of China. The song goes through the months of the year, and compares the wife's life to her neighbors whose husbands are home. This Han song is from Jiangsu province.

CRESCENT MOON (page 17)

This is a sad song. The crescent moon is seen across the country reminding people that some families are together while others are apart. This Han song is from Jiangsu province.

BLUE FLOWER (page 18)

This song is about a young girl who is very upset about the prospects of an arranged marriage. She secretly desires to run away with her true lover. This Han song is from Shaanxi province.

DIGGING FOR POTATOES (page 19)

This funny song refers to actually the eddo, or taro root, which is a potato-like root. In this song a man is digging for an eddo and instead uncovers a grasshopper! This Han song is from Shanxi province.

WOVEN BASKET (page 20)

The song's title refers to the baskets used in carrying labor. This Han song originates from the Zhejiang province.

BEATING THE WILD HOG (page 21)

The hog is a nuisance animal because it eats the farmers' plants. The men gather and set out to kill the wild hog. This Han song is from Zhejiang province.

LITTLE COWHERD (page 22)

A young cowherd boasts that he knows many things because he asks many questions. This Han song is from Hebei province.

CARRYING SONG (page 24)
This Han song from Shaanxi province is about happy traveling.

MEMORIAL (page 26)
In this Korean song from Jilin province, a woman goes out to pick vegetables in the field, but she is actually gathering flowers to put on her lover's tomb. With a poignant phrase wrought with irony she exclaims, "It's hard to dig you up."

HAND DRUM SONG (page 28)
This Han song from Anhui province reflects on a difficult existence. The beggar says, "In tough times rich people sell their donkeys and poor people sell their children. I don't have any children so you find me on the street playing my drum [for money]."

SONG OF THE CLOWN (page 30)
A clown sings this comedic song in the opera. The Han people in Taiwan sing this song.

JASMINE FLOWER (page 32)
The allegory of the jasmine flower symbolizing a girl is a very common subject (and title) in Chinese songs. This Han song is from Jiangsu province.

DARKENING SKY (page 34)
In this Han song the sky is dark and it's going to rain. The men are digging up roots in the field and find an eel in the water! They kill it and take it home to cook it. Grandpa wants salt and grandma disagrees. They fight over how to cook it, and the pots go "ding-dong" until they finally break. This song is from Taiwan.

NORTHWEST RAINS (page 40)
This Taiwanese children's song is about torrential rains on the island. The song has fun, silly words as it warns farmers to get out of the fields because eels (snake-like fish common in Asian rice fields) will come out to "play their drums" during the rains.

HOMESICK (page 42)
In this song, farmers deliver food to different places while being away from home for three years. This Han song is from Shaanxi province.

MOUNTAINTOP VIEW

沂蒙山好風光

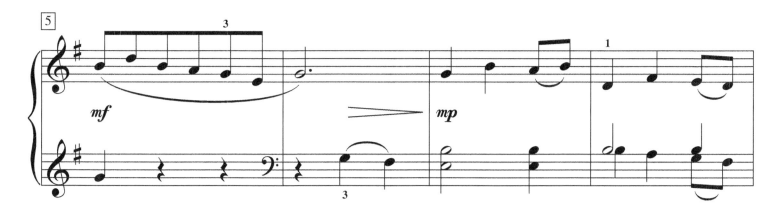

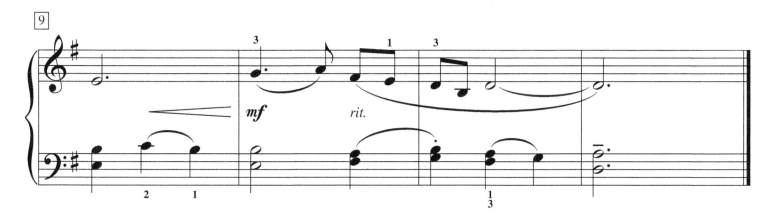

LOVE SONG OF THE PRAIRIE
草原情歌

RUNNING HORSE MOUNTAIN

跑馬溜溜的山上

GIRL'S LAMENT
信天游

WEDDING VEIL

掀起你的蓋頭來

SAD, RAINY DAY

落水天

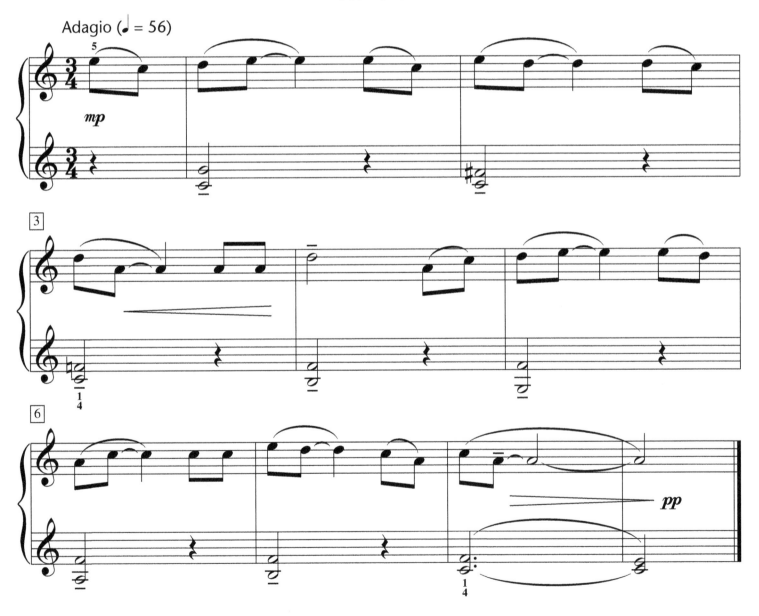

THE SUN CAME UP HAPPY
太陽出來喜洋洋

Allegretto (♩ = 96)

WA-HA-HA!
哇哈哈

WHITE FLOWER

栀子開花白又白

GREAT WALL

孟姜女

CRESCENT MOON
月兒彎彎照九州

BLUE FLOWER
藍花花

DIGGING FOR POTATOES

刨洋芋

WOVEN BASKET

做簍歌

BEATING THE WILD HOG

打野豬

LITTLE COWHERD

小放牛

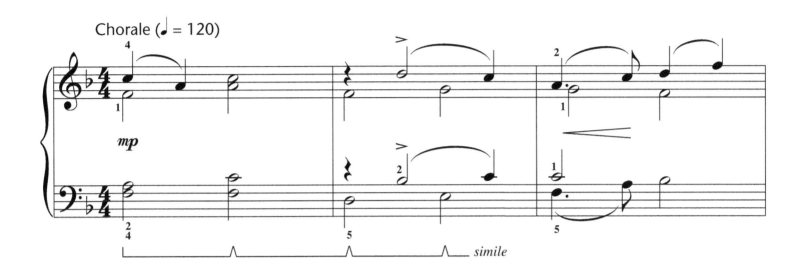

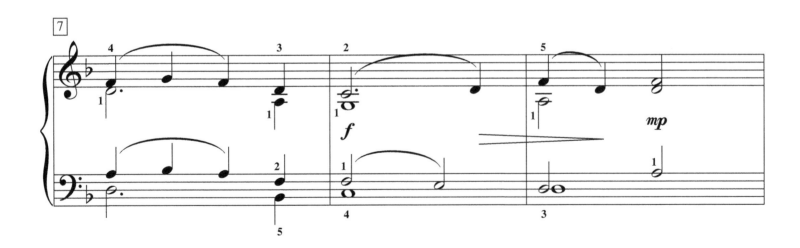

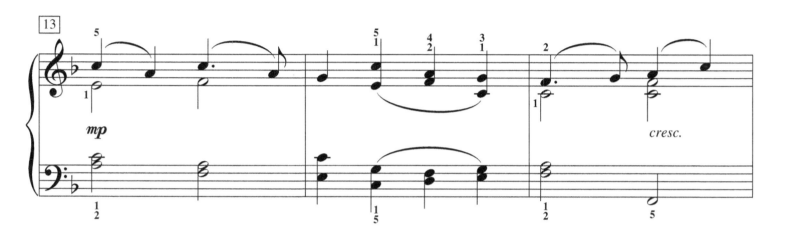

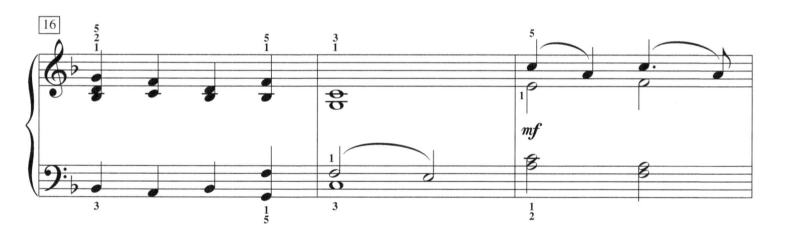

CARRYING SONG

走絳州

Energetic (♩ = 92)

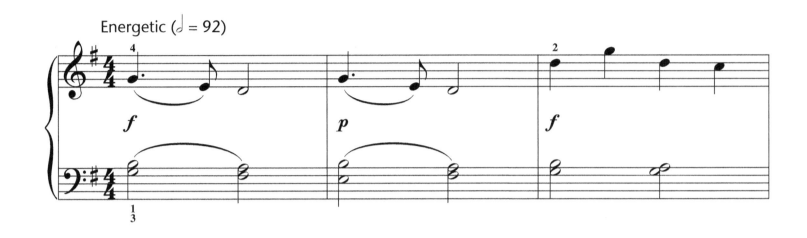

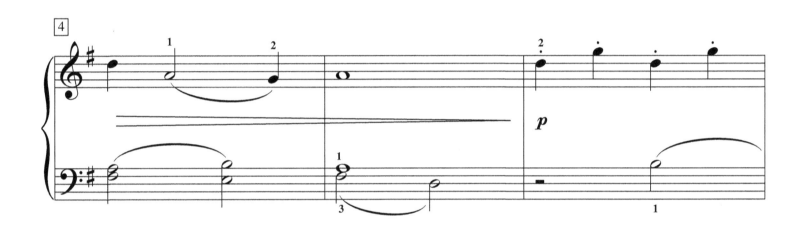

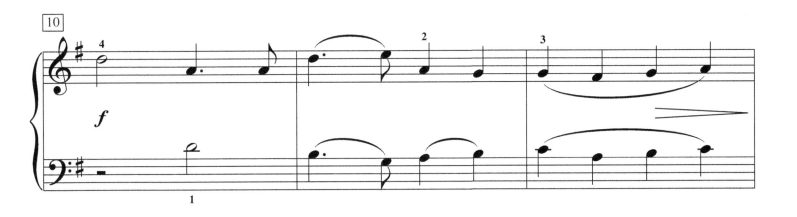

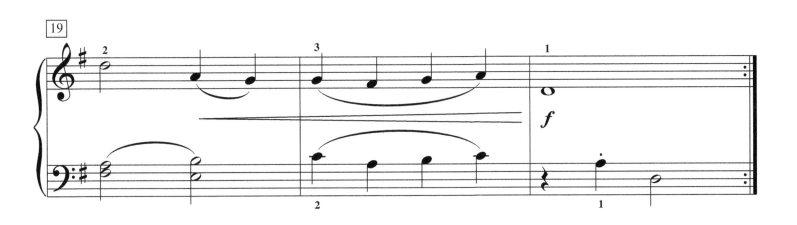

MEMORIAL
道拉基

HAND DRUM SONG
鳳陽花鼓

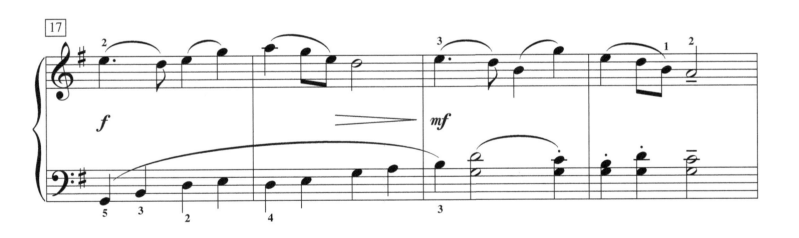

SONG OF THE CLOWN

丟丟銅

Moderato (♩ = 88)

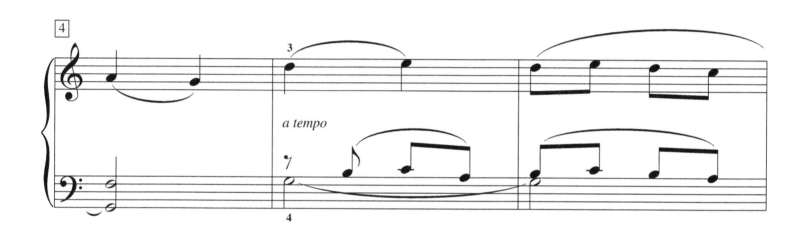

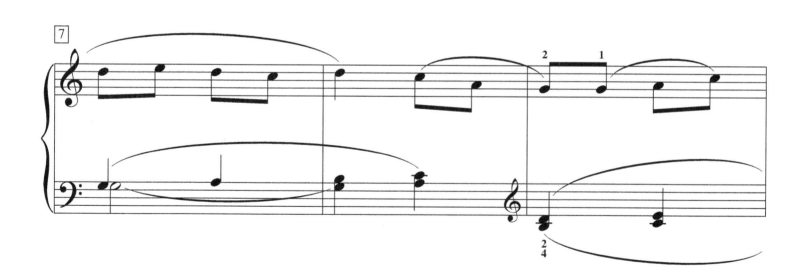

JASMINE FLOWER

茉莉花

DARKENING SKY
天鳥鳥

Moderately (♩ = 100)

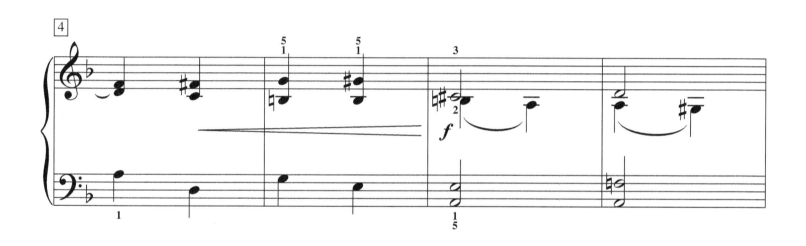

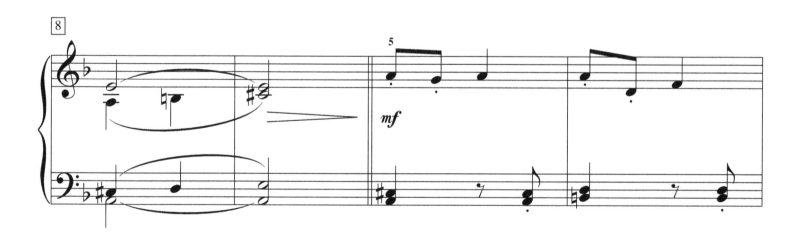

NORTHWEST RAINS

西北雨直直落

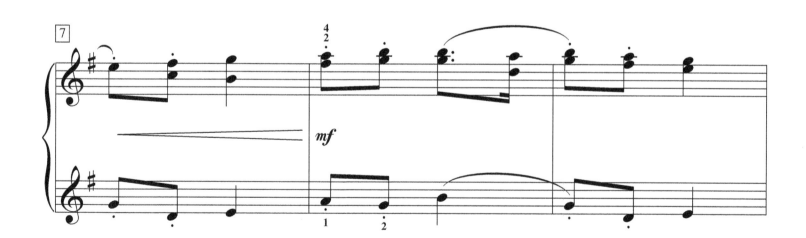

HOMESICK
(THEME AND FIVE VARIATIONS)

脚夫調

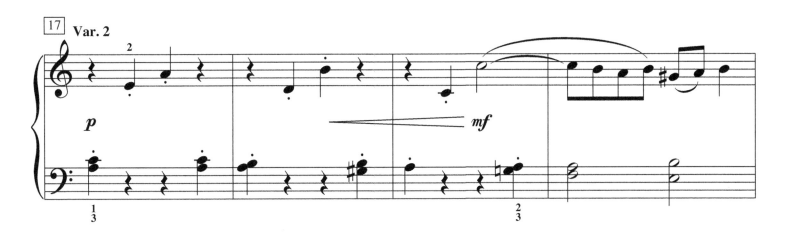

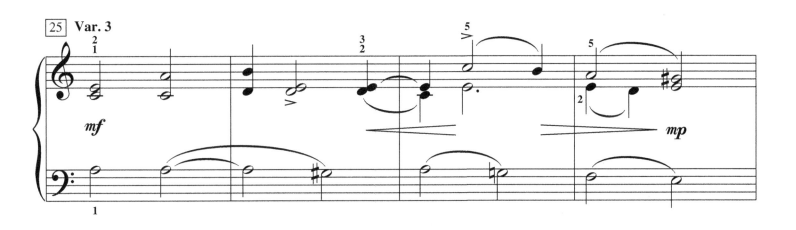

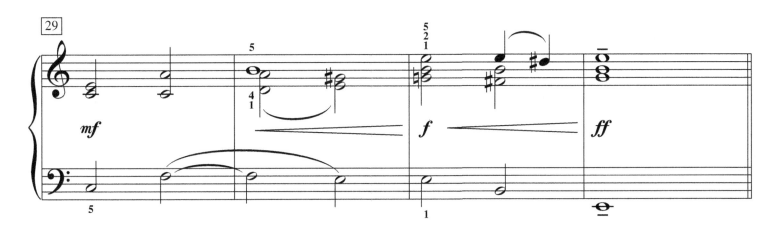

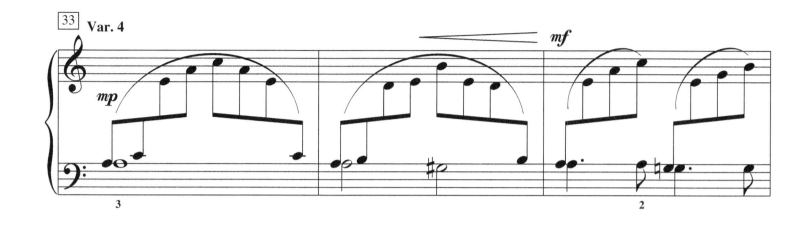

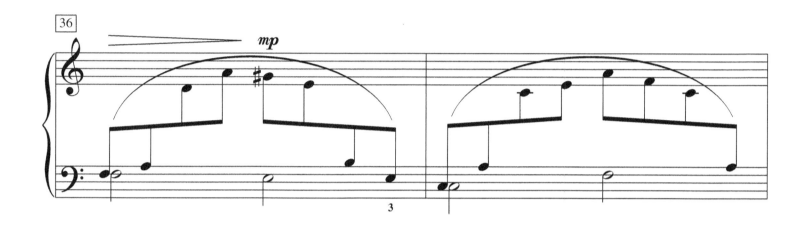

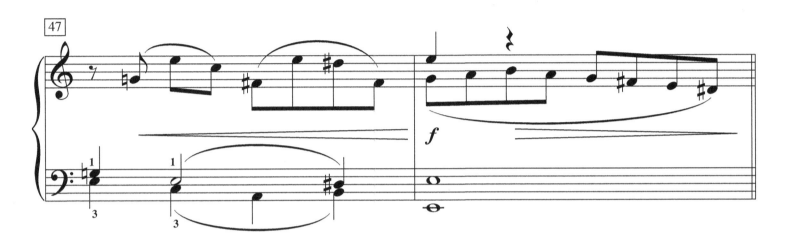

Coda (Theme reprise)

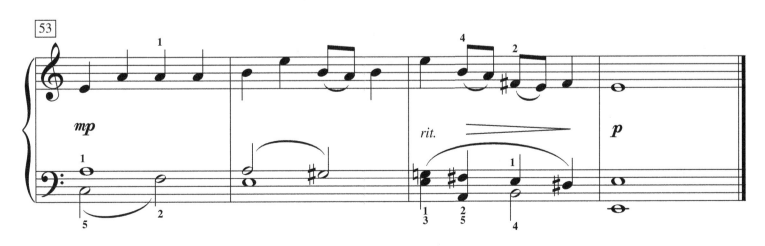

FOLK SONG COLLECTIONS
FOR PIANO SOLO

Introduce piano students to the music of world cultures with folk songs arranged for intermediate piano solo. Each collection features 24 folk songs and includes detailed notes about the folk songs, beautiful illustrations, as well as a map of the regions.

AFRICAN AMERICAN

arr. Artina McCain

The Bamboula · By and By · Deep River · Didn't My Lord Deliver Daniel? · Don't You Let Nobody Turn You Around · Every Time I Feel the Spirit · Give Me That Old Time Religion · Guide My Feet · I Want Jesus to Walk With Me · I Was Way Down A-Yonder · I'm a Soldier, Let Me Ride · In Bright Mansions Above · Lift Ev'ry Voice and Sing · Little David, Play on Your Harp · My Lord, What a Morning · Ride On, King Jesus · Run Mary Run · Sometimes I Feel Like a Motherless Child · Song of Conquest · Take Nabandji · Wade in the Water · Warriors' Song · Watch and Pray · What a Beautiful City.
00358084 Piano Solo..$12.99

IRISH

arr. June Armstrong

As I Walked Out One Morning · Ballinderry · Blind Mary · Bunclody · Carrickfergus · The Castle of Dromore (The October Winds) · The Cliffs of Doneen · The Coolin · Courtin' in the Kitchen · Down Among the Ditches O · Down by the Salley Gardens · The Fairy Woman of Lough Leane · Follow Me Up to Carlow · The Gartan Mother's Lullaby · Huish the Cat · I'll Tell My Ma · Kitty of Coleraine · The Londonderry Air · My Lagan Love · My Love Is an Arbutus · Rocky Road to Dublin · Slieve Gallion Braes · Squire Parsons · That Night in Bethlehem.
00234359 Piano Solo..$12.99

MALAY
(MALAYSIAN AND INDONESIAN)

arr. Charmaine Siagian

At Dawn · Chan Mali Chan · C'mon, Mama! · The Cockatoo · The Curvy Water Spinach Stalk · Five Little Chicks · God Bless the Sultan · The Goodbye Song · Great Indonesia · It's All Good Here · The Jumping Frog · Longing · Mak Inang · Milk Coffee · The Moon Kite · Morning Tide · My Country · Onward Singapore · Ponyfish · Song for the Ladybugs · The Stork Song · Suriram · Trek Tek Tek · Voyage of the Sampan.
00288420 Piano Solo..$10.99

CHINESE

arr. Joseph Johnson

Beating the Wild Hog · Blue Flower · Carrying Song · Crescent Moon · Darkening Sky · Digging for Potatoes · Girl's Lament · Great Wall · Hand Drum Song · Homesick · Jasmine Flower Song · Little Cowherd · Love Song of the Prarie · Memorial · Mountaintop View · Northwest Rains · Running Horse Mountain · Sad, Rainy Day · Song of the Clown · The Sun Came Up Happy · Wa-Ha-Ha · Wedding Veil · White Flower · Woven Basket.
00296764 Piano Solo..$12.99

KOREAN

arr. Lawrence Lee

Arirang · Autumn in the City · Birdie, Birdie · Boat Song · Catch the Tail · Chestnut · Cricket · Dance in the Moonlight · Five Hundred Years · Flowers · Fun Is Here · The Gate · Han River · Harvest · Jindo Field Song · Lullaby · The Mill · The Palace · The Pier · Three-Way Junction · Waterfall · Wild Herbs · Yearning · You and I.
00296810 Piano Solo..$12.99

JAPANESE

arr. Mika Goto

Blooming Flowers · Come Here, Fireflies · Counting Game · The Fisherman's Song · Going to the Shrine · Harvest Song · Itsuki Lullaby · Joyful Doll Festival · Kimigayo · Let's Sing · My Hometown · Picking Tea Leaves · The Rabbit on the Moon · Rain · Rain Showers · Rock-Paper-Scissors · Sakura · Seven Baby Crows · Takeda Lullaby · Time to Go Home · Village Festival · Where Are You From? · Wish I Could Go · You're It!
00296891 Piano Solo..$12.99

SOUTH AFRICAN

arr. James Wilding, Nkululeko Zungu

The Axe Cuts the Thorn Tree · The Clouds They Thunder ·The Crowing of the Rooster · The Doves Above · God Bless Africa · Here Comes the Alibama · I Have a Sweetheart in Durban · Jan Pierewiet · Mama, Who Is This? · Our Dearest Mothers · Sarie Marais · Sugar Bush · They Say There's a Man in the Moon · What Have We Done? · and more!
00368666 Piano Solo $12.99

HAL•LEONARD®

halleonard.com

*Prices, contents and availability
subject to change without notice.*

MAP OF CHINA

Heilongjiang Province

Jilin Province

Liaoning Province

Inner Mongolia Autonomous Region

Shanghai

Taiwan

Zhejiang Province

Hong Kong S.A.R.

Macau S.A.R.

Tianjin

Beijing

Shandong Province

Jiangsu Province

Anhui Province

Fujian Province

Hebei Province

Jiangxi Province

Guangdong Province

Shanxi Province

Henan Province

Hubei Province

Hunan Province

Ningxia Hui Autonomous Region

Shaanxi Province

Chongqing

Guizhou Province

Guangxi Zhuang Autonomous Region

Hainan Province

Gansu Province

Sichuan Province

Yunnan Province

Qinghai Province

Xinjiang Province

Tibet Autonomous Region

COMPOSER SHOWCASE
HAL LEONARD STUDENT PIANO LIBRARY

This series showcases great original piano music from our **Hal Leonard Student Piano Library** family of composers. Carefully graded for easy selection.

BILL BOYD

JAZZ BITS (AND PIECES)
Early Intermediate Level
00290312 11 Solos......................$7.99

JAZZ DELIGHTS
Intermediate Level
00240435 11 Solos......................$8.99

JAZZ FEST
Intermediate Level
00240436 10 Solos......................$8.99

JAZZ PRELIMS
Early Elementary Level
00290032 12 Solos......................$7.99

JAZZ SKETCHES
Intermediate Level
00220001 8 Solos......................$8.99

JAZZ STARTERS
Elementary Level
00290425 10 Solos......................$8.99

JAZZ STARTERS II
Late Elementary Level
00290434 11 Solos......................$7.99

JAZZ STARTERS III
Late Elementary Level
00290465 12 Solos......................$8.99

THINK JAZZ!
Early Intermediate Level
00290417 Method Book............$12.99

TONY CARAMIA

JAZZ MOODS
Intermediate Level
00296728 8 Solos......................$6.95

SUITE DREAMS
Intermediate Level
00296775 4 Solos......................$6.99

SONDRA CLARK

DAKOTA DAYS
Intermediate Level
00296521 5 Solos......................$6.95

FLORIDA FANTASY SUITE
Intermediate Level
00296766 3 Duets......................$7.95

THREE ODD METERS
Intermediate Level
00296472 3 Duets......................$6.95

MATTHEW EDWARDS

CONCERTO FOR YOUNG PIANISTS
FOR 2 PIANOS, FOUR HANDS
Intermediate Level Book/CD
00296356 3 Movements $19.99

CONCERTO NO. 2 IN G MAJOR
FOR 2 PIANOS, 4 HANDS
Intermediate Level Book/CD
00296670 3 Movements............$17.99

PHILLIP KEVEREN

MOUSE ON A MIRROR
Late Elementary Level
00296361 5 Solos......................$8.99

MUSICAL MOODS
Elementary/Late Elementary Level
00296714 7 Solos......................$6.99

SHIFTY-EYED BLUES
Late Elementary Level
00296374 5 Solos......................$7.99

CAROL KLOSE

THE BEST OF CAROL KLOSE
Early to Late Intermediate Level
00146151 15 Solos...................$12.99

CORAL REEF SUITE
Late Elementary Level
00296354 7 Solos......................$7.50

DESERT SUITE
Intermediate Level
00296667 6 Solos......................$7.99

FANCIFUL WALTZES
Early Intermediate Level
00296473 5 Solos......................$7.95

GARDEN TREASURES
Late Intermediate Level
00296787 5 Solos......................$8.50

ROMANTIC EXPRESSIONS
Intermediate to Late Intermediate Level
00296923 5 Solos......................$8.99

WATERCOLOR MINIATURES
Early Intermediate Level
00296848 7 Solos......................$7.99

JENNIFER LINN

AMERICAN IMPRESSIONS
Intermediate Level
00296471 6 Solos......................$8.99

ANIMALS HAVE FEELINGS TOO
Early Elementary/Elementary Level
00147789 8 Solos......................$8.99

AU CHOCOLAT
Late Elementary/Early Intermediate Level
00298110 7 Solos......................$8.99

CHRISTMAS IMPRESSIONS
Intermediate Level
00296706 8 Solos......................$8.99

JUST PINK
Elementary Level
00296722 9 Solos......................$8.99

LES PETITES IMAGES
Late Elementary Level
00296664 7 Solos......................$8.99

LES PETITES IMPRESSIONS
Intermediate Level
00296355 6 Solos......................$8.99

REFLECTIONS
Late Intermediate Level
00296843 5 Solos......................$8.99

TALES OF MYSTERY
Intermediate Level
00296769 6 Solos......................$8.99

LYNDA LYBECK-ROBINSON

ALASKA SKETCHES
Early Intermediate Level
00119637 8 Solos......................$8.99

AN AWESOME ADVENTURE
Late Elementary Level
00137563 8 Solos......................$7.99

FOR THE BIRDS
Early Intermediate/Intermediate Level
00237078 9 Solos......................$8.99

WHISPERING WOODS
Late Elementary Level
00275905 9 Solos......................$8.99

MONA REJINO

CIRCUS SUITE
Late Elementary Level
00296665 5 Solos......................$8.99

COLOR WHEEL
Early Intermediate Level
00201951 6 Solos......................$9.99

IMPRESIONES DE ESPAÑA
Intermediate Level
00337520 6 Solos......................$8.99

IMPRESSIONS OF NEW YORK
Intermediate Level
00364212......................$8.99

JUST FOR KIDS
Elementary Level
00296840 8 Solos......................$7.99

MERRY CHRISTMAS MEDLEYS
Intermediate Level
00296799 5 Solos......................$8.99

MINIATURES IN STYLE
Intermediate Level
00148088 6 Solos......................$8.99

PORTRAITS IN STYLE
Early Intermediate Level
00296507 6 Solos......................$8.99

EUGÉNIE ROCHEROLLE

CELEBRATION SUITE
Intermediate Level
00152724 3 Duets......................$8.99

ENCANTOS ESPAÑOLES (SPANISH DELIGHTS)
Intermediate Level
00125451 6 Solos......................$8.99

JAMBALAYA
Intermediate Level
00296654 2 Pianos, 8 Hands.....$12.99
00296725 2 Pianos, 4 Hands.......$7.95

JEROME KERN CLASSICS
Intermediate Level
00296577 10 Solos...................$12.99

LITTLE BLUES CONCERTO
Early Intermediate Level
00142801 2 Pianos, 4 Hands......$12.99

TOUR FOR TWO
Late Elementary Level
00296832 6 Duets......................$9.99

TREASURES
Late Elementary/Early Intermediate Level
00296924 7 Solos......................$8.99

JEREMY SISKIND

BIG APPLE JAZZ
Intermediate Level
00278209 8 Solos......................$8.99

MYTHS AND MONSTERS
Late Elementary/Early Intermediate Level
00148148 9 Solos......................$8.99

CHRISTOS TSITSAROS

DANCES FROM AROUND THE WORLD
Early Intermediate Level
00296688 7 Solos......................$8.99

FIVE SUMMER PIECES
Late Intermediate/Advanced Level
00361235 5 Solos...................$12.99

LYRIC BALLADS
Intermediate/Late Intermediate Level
00102404 6 Solos......................$8.99

POETIC MOMENTS
Intermediate Level
00296403 8 Solos......................$8.99

SEA DIARY
Early Intermediate Level
00253486 9 Solos......................$8.99

SONATINA HUMORESQUE
Late Intermediate Level
00296772 3 Movements..............$6.99

SONGS WITHOUT WORDS
Intermediate Level
00296506 9 Solos......................$9.99

THREE PRELUDES
Early Advanced Level
00130747 3 Solos......................$8.99

THROUGHOUT THE YEAR
Late Elementary Level
00296723 12 Duets......................$6.95

ADDITIONAL COLLECTIONS

AT THE LAKE
by Elvina Pearce
Elementary/Late Elementary Level
00131642 10 Solos and Duets.....$7.99

CHRISTMAS FOR TWO
by Dan Fox
Early Intermediate Level
00290069 13 Duets...................$8.99

CHRISTMAS JAZZ
by Mike Springer
Intermediate Level
00296525 6 Solos......................$8.99

COUNTY RAGTIME FESTIVAL
by Fred Kern
Intermediate Level
00296882 7 Solos......................$7.99

LITTLE JAZZERS
by Jennifer Watts
Elementary/Late Elementary Level
00154573 9 Solos......................$8.99

PLAY THE BLUES!
by Luann Carman
Early Intermediate Level
00296357 10 Solos......................$9.99

ROLLER COASTERS & RIDES
by Jennifer & Mike Watts
Intermediate Level
00131144 8 Duets......................$8.99

HAL•LEONARD®
www.halleonard.com

Prices, contents, and availability subject to change without notice.